Ferry Crossing

Published by 99% Press,
an imprint of Lasavia Publishing Ltd.
Auckland, New Zealand
www.lasaviapublishing.com

ISBN 978-0-9951398-8-6

Ferry Crossing

Leila Lees

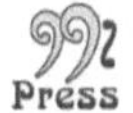

Press

In 2010 my mother died after a long period of illness with alzheimers. Ferry crossing was written during the time of her dying. It was during this time that I began to draw. My mother was a watercolour artist and I inherited her art materials. I wrote and drew in a small notebook as I travelled on a ferry from Waiheke to Auckland and back. This poem is dedicated to my mother, for her keen observation of nature, her ascetic sense of beauty and her courage.

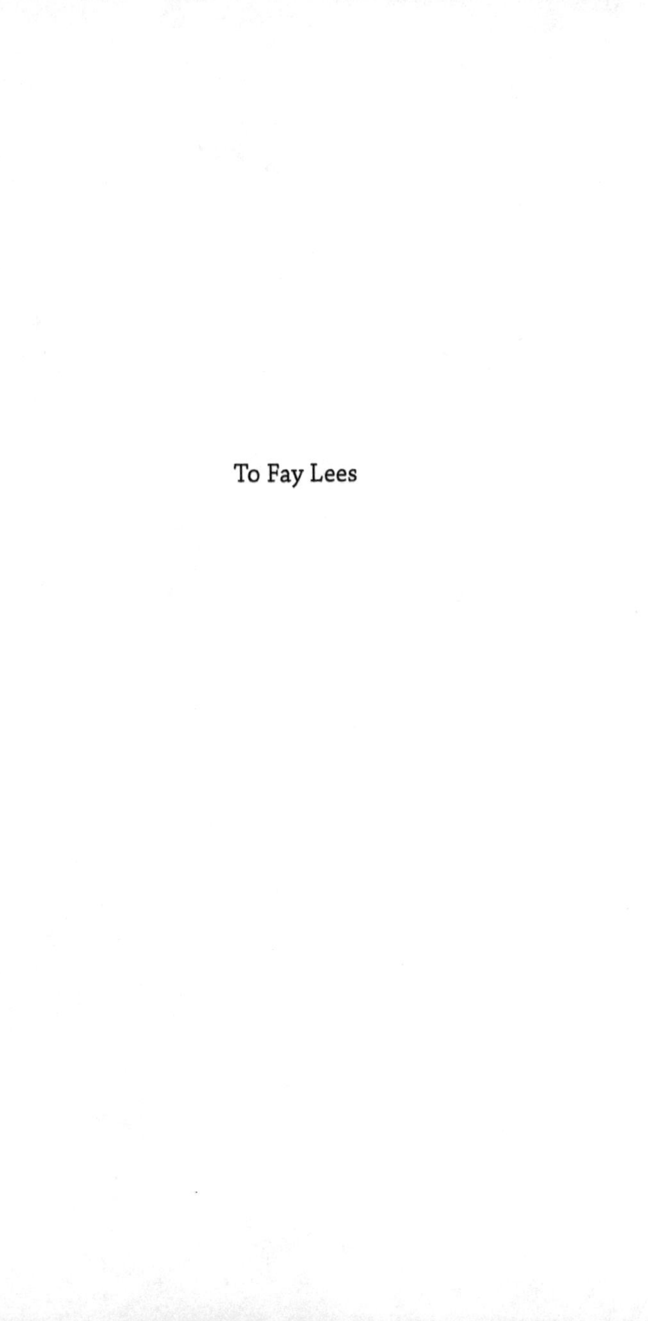

To Fay Lees

Ferry Crossing

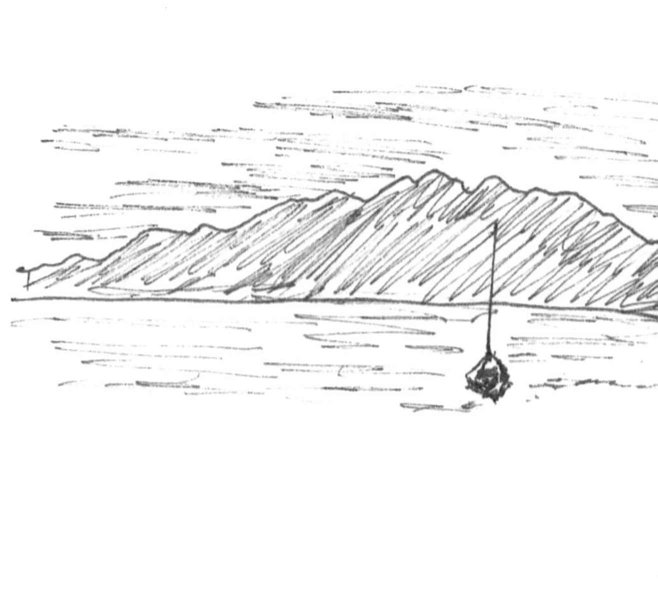

bit by bit

we lose you

together

sunglasses to the wind

my tears dry on the asphalt

I choose

to sit outside

looking back

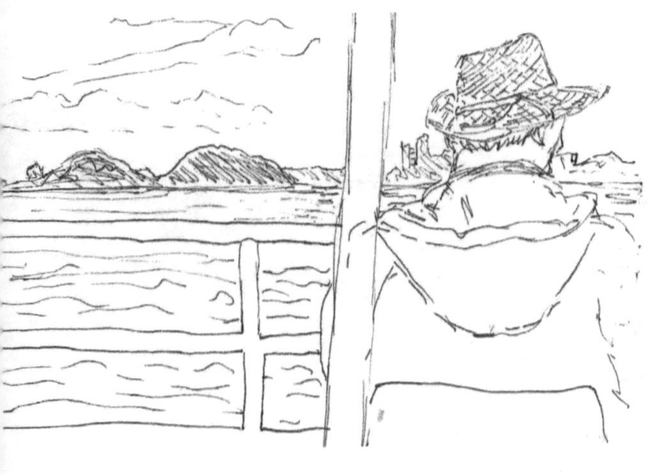

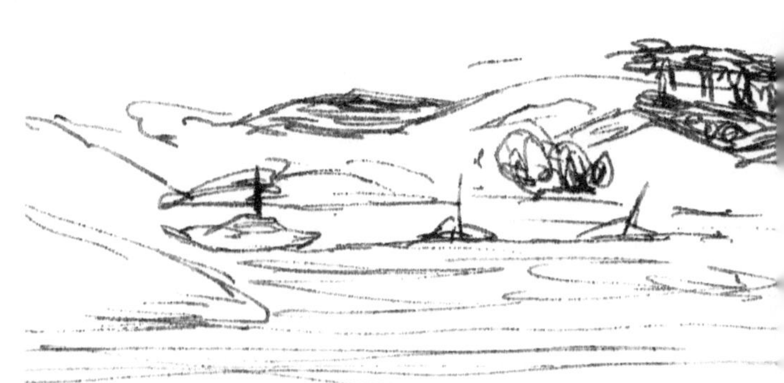

the large stingray
is almost
at the same place

there is a cloud
in front of a cloud
as if it shouldn't belong
there

a little bit of a swell out here

clay cliffs of motutapu

one gull flying
on a mission

three men rocking in a boat
fishing

kayaks
in the wake

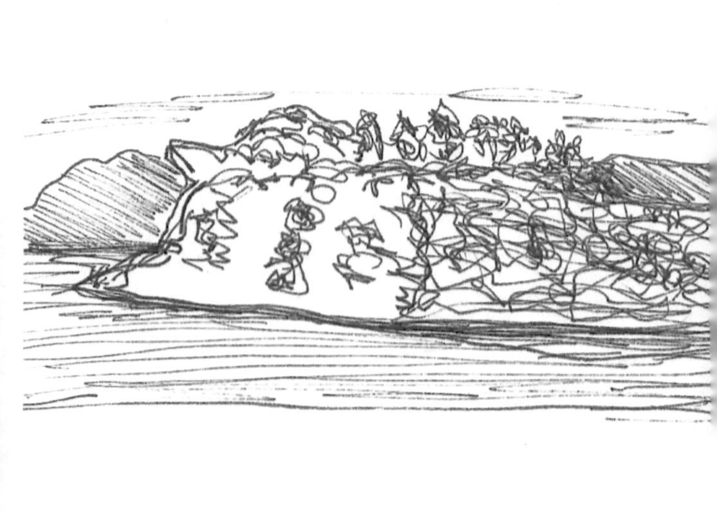

I lie in bed waking
to the drift of dawn through the gaps made
by the curtain and the smell
of the sheets left in the rain too long

in the ghost light
tiny white moths hover
and flutter in the water colour sky

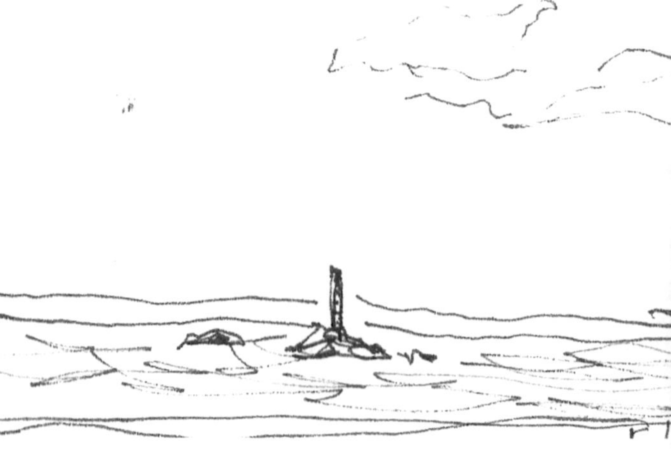

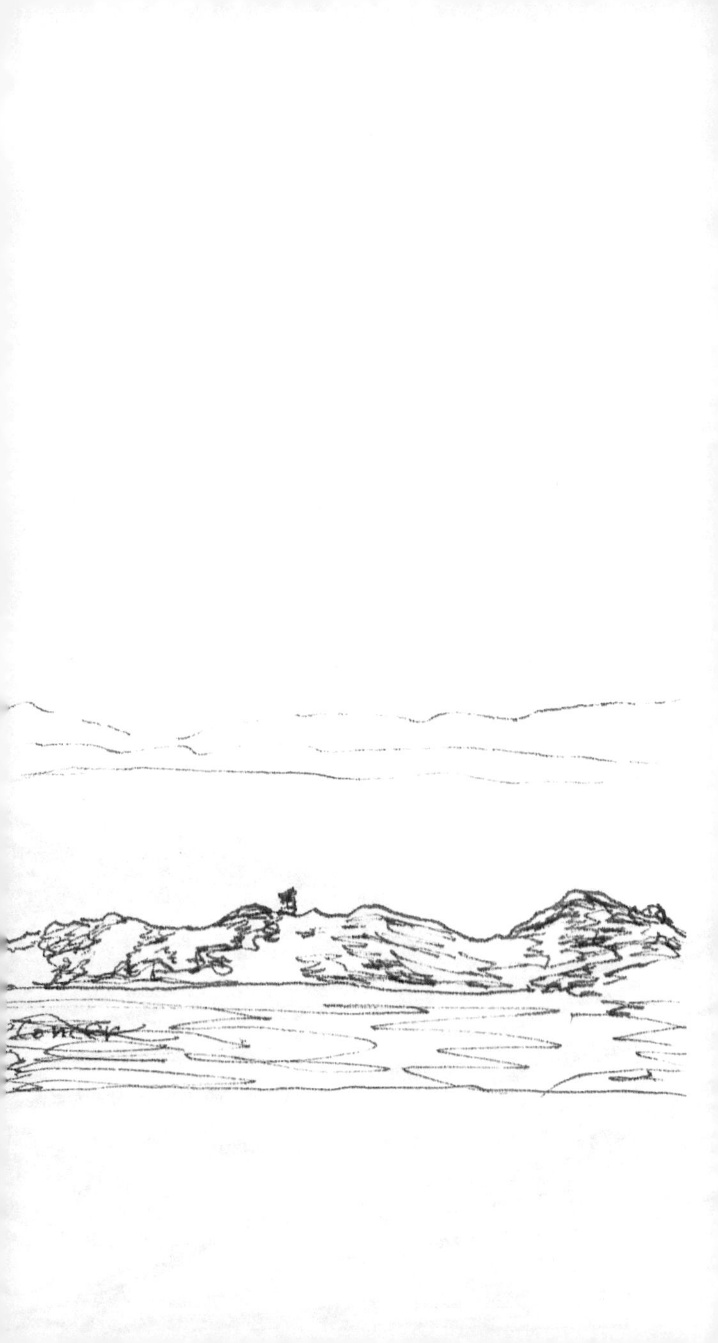

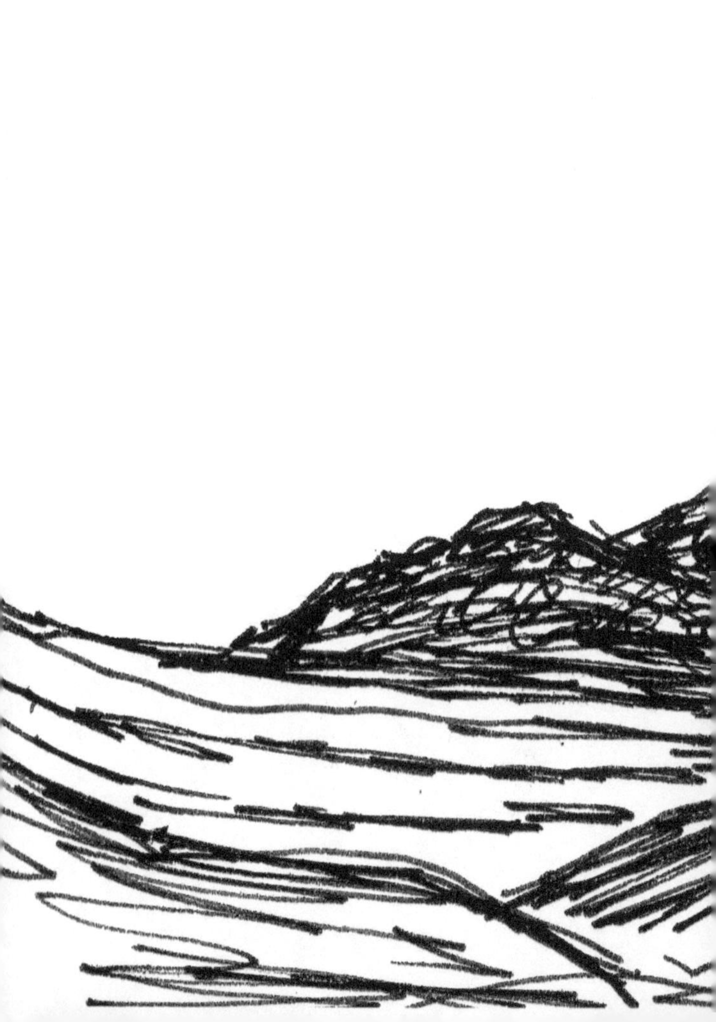

the seats have holes

in storms

the water can wash through

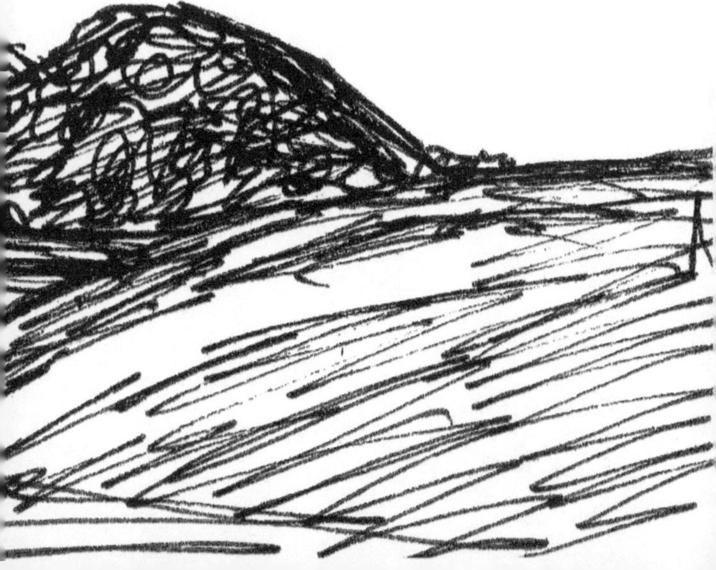

the chair, the space, the table
a white page

Graphite_ Charcoal_ Pencils

materials you leave behind

a charcoal rubber
put into a film canister

EE Lumograph

missing
a small ruler
in my pencil case

practise scales of shading

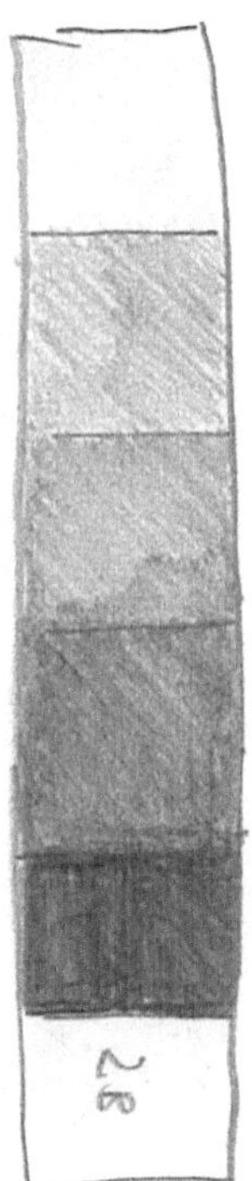

rangitoto invisible
in the night
I place the kernel
in the hidden cradle
gently rocking

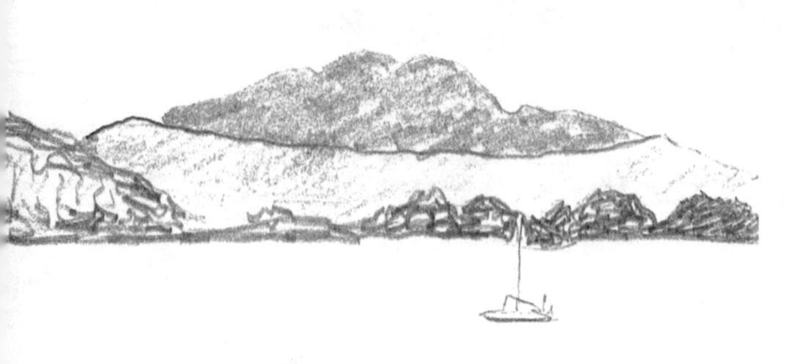

Looking at Rangitoto through from the other side of
motutapu. from the ferry

light and shadow
on the hills – go out of rhythm

a bit of wind out here

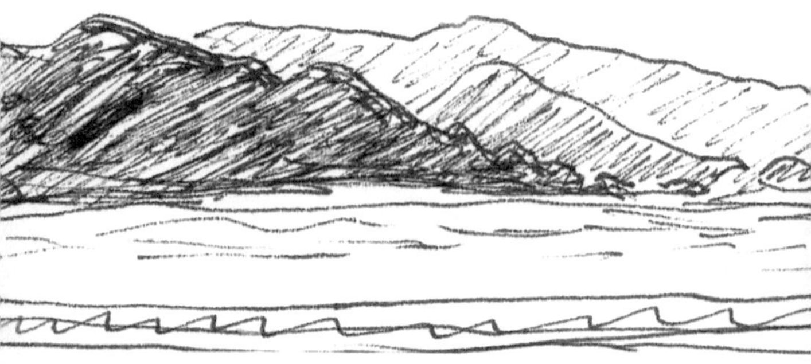

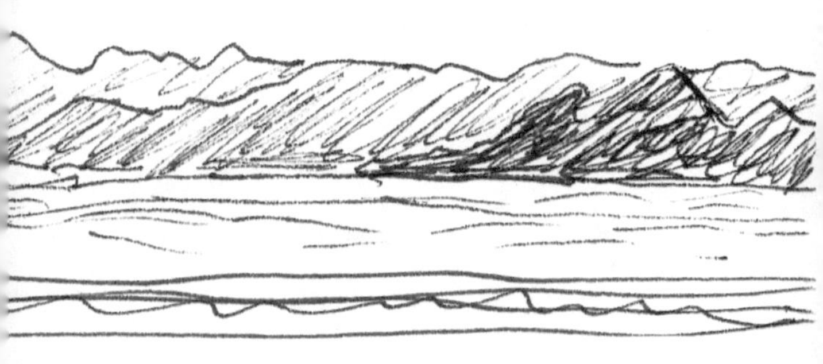

art materials strewn loosely

no knowing how

anymore

draw
first the line on the horizon

foregrounds
packed

or restfully blank

hills above matiatia
5b pencil

motuihe island
2b pencil

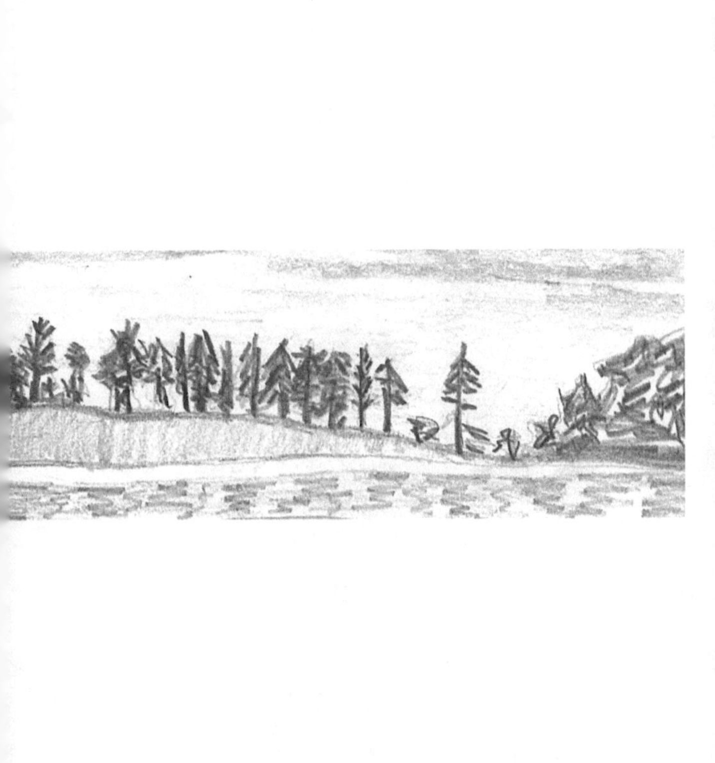

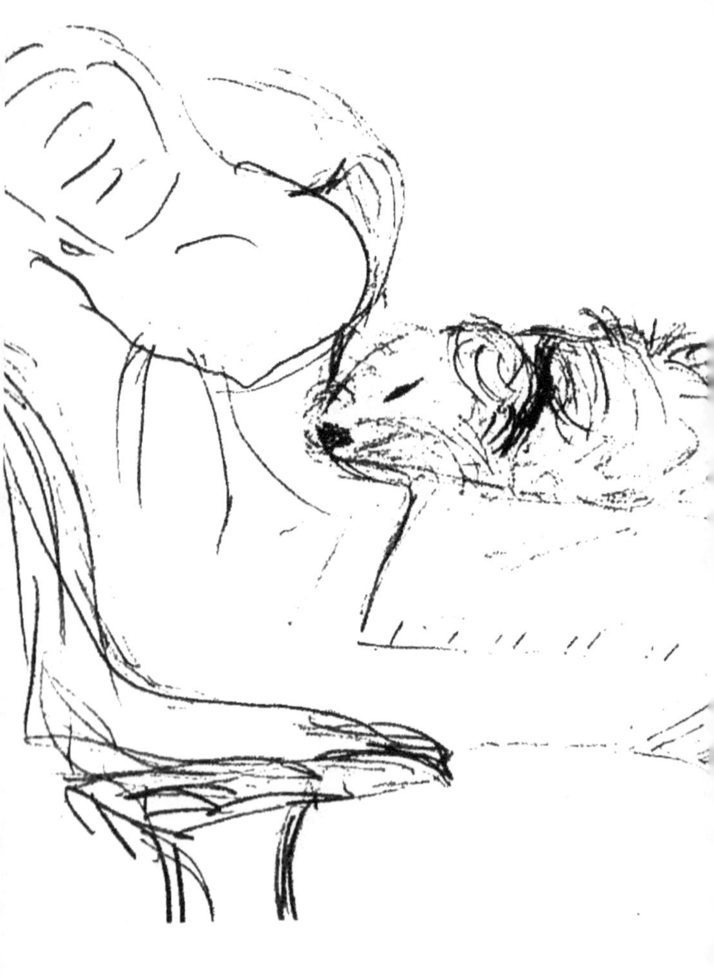

19 Sept. Overcast – No rain.
sleeping dog on man's knees.
coming into the city now

old fabric
tears

I hold your hand

looking the other way
wondering how to be

with small shreds

start drawing
anywhere

shadow hills
lose definition

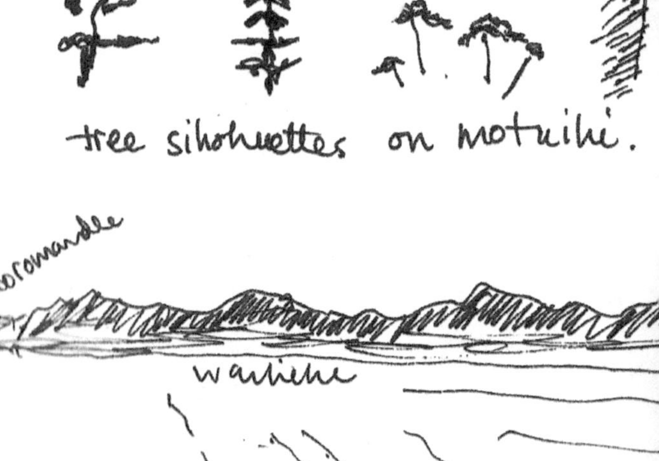

and still in the night

I see

the trees

silhouette

Browns Island

waiheke channel
A star above the moon
venus
Waiheke silohuething
pohutukawa
that blue
   and the orange sunrise
turning boat now
with motutapu on my side

Thinking that I'm understanding
slowing the sketch book – would
still like to create a black paper
and some different paper
zoo sketchbook.
How can I create time to do that?

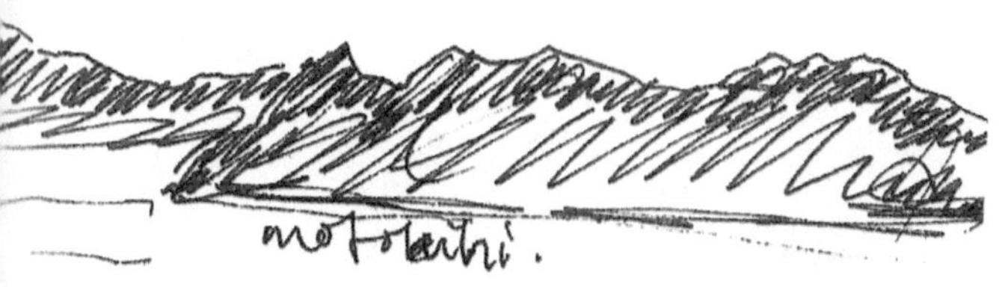

there's a star

one

in _ between the winged

clouds

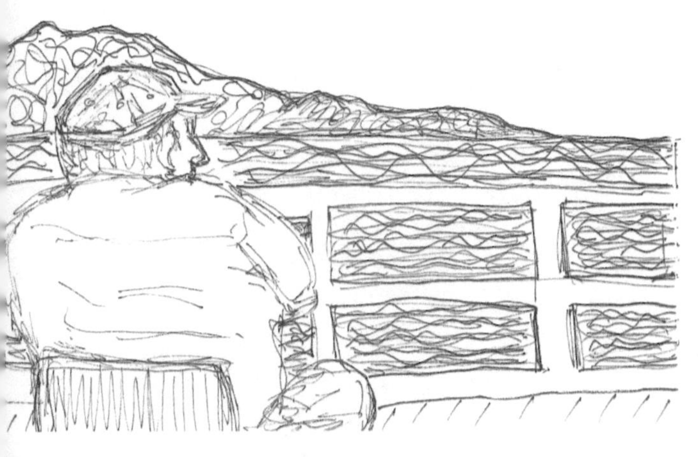

observing the people around me wondering
the etiquette of drawing people.

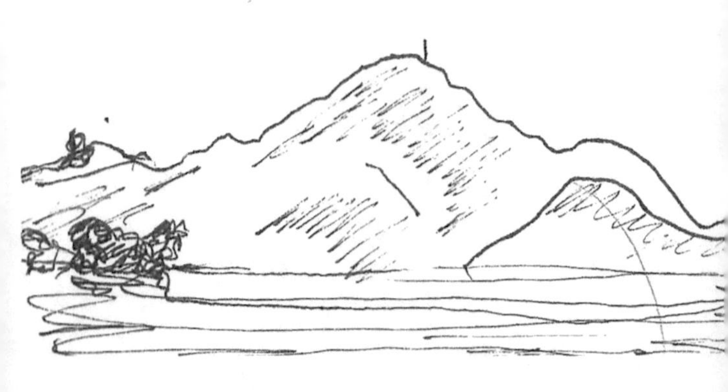

one star
then another
the sky black
the water inky and rippling

mute and fragile,
the spoon too big for your mouth

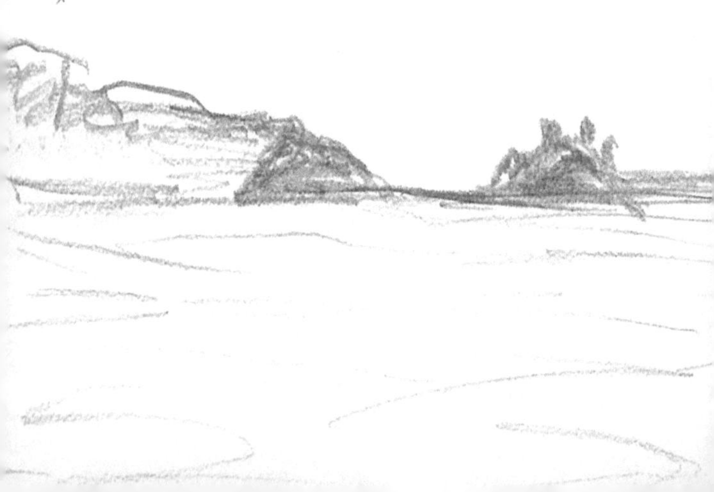

I am the clumsy giant

I rush the door to the sky

while the nurse lifts you into a wheel chair

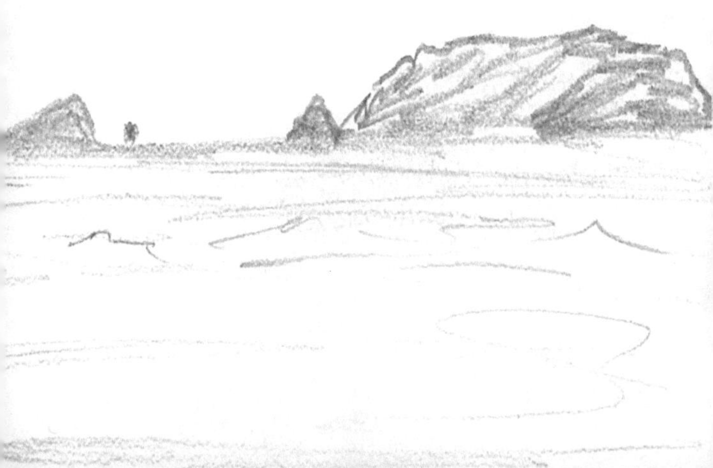

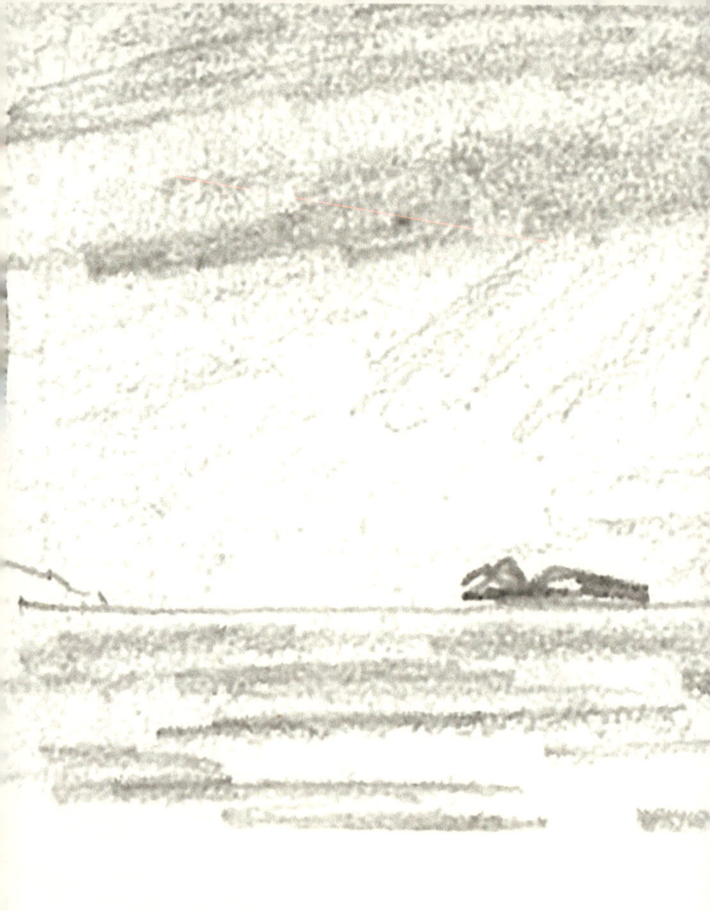

words are uncertain

they are lifted back
to their unformed
space

they spill toward

some other meaning

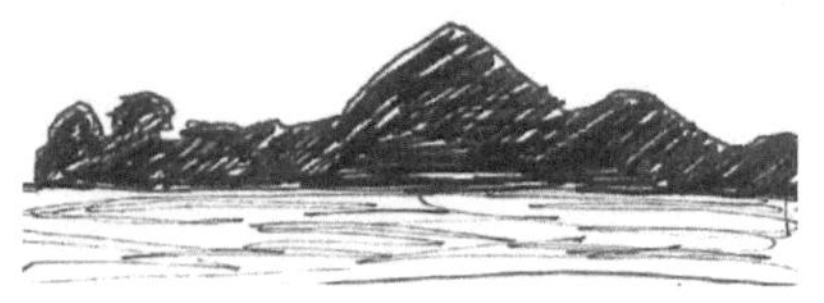

Coromandel
softens behind the cloud

Motutapu
The yellow - steep cliffs ripple
In contrast to the green tops

Motukorea
when light
bathes the object from one side
there is a point
at which the light stops
and becomes a shadow

bean rock
drawing it
closer and

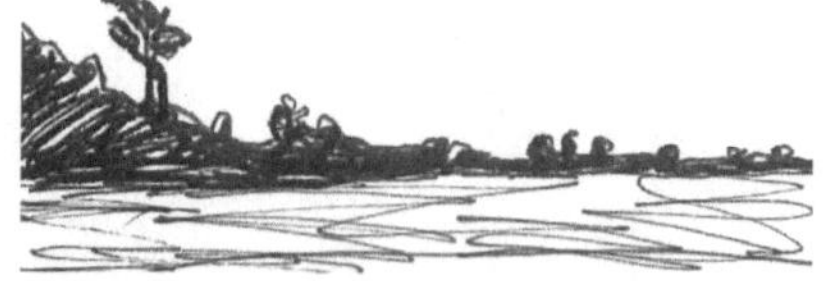

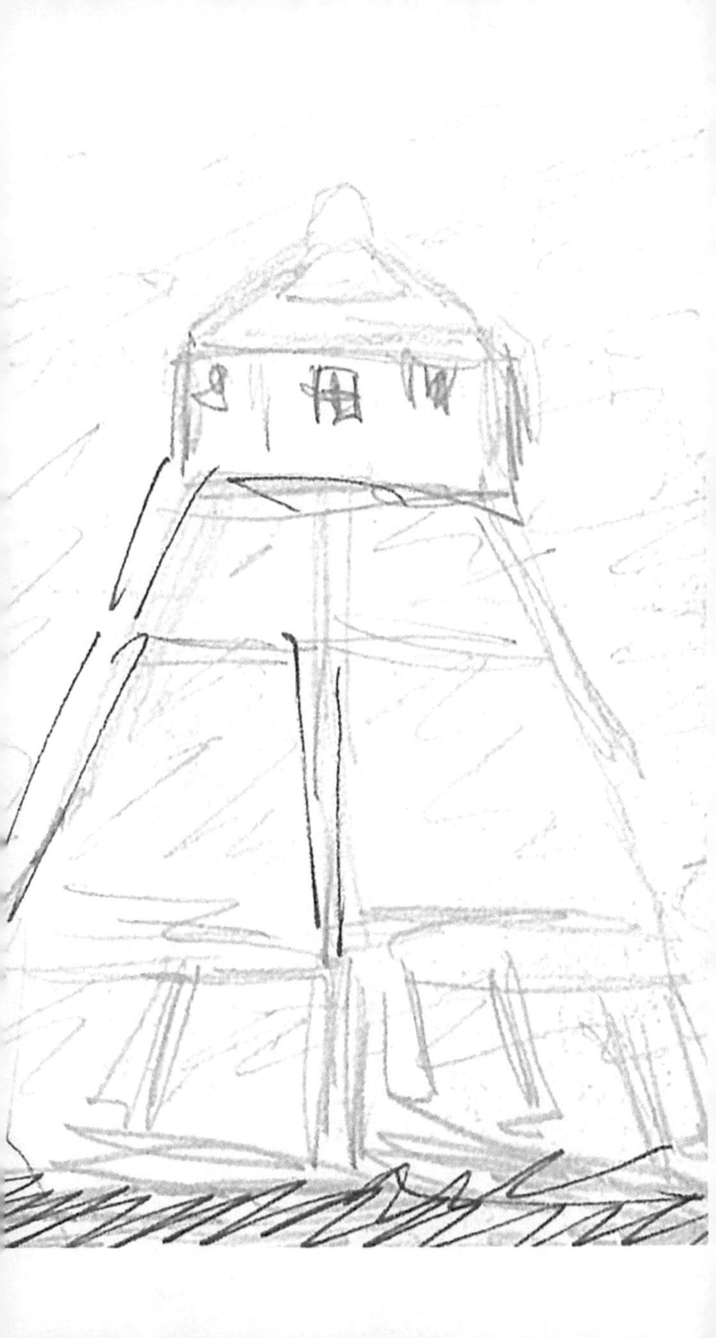

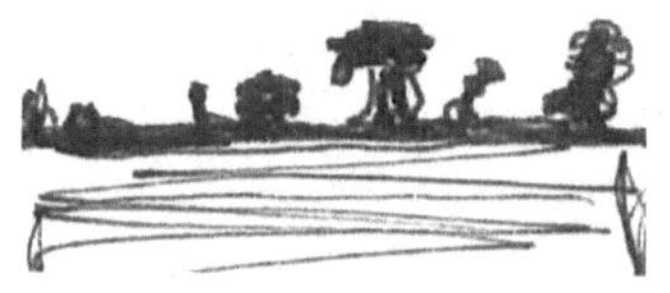

motukorea 7 a.m
7th July

Looking back
Looking forward
Looking back

autumn wind
a dry leaf on the pavement

waiting for the taxi

how do I wait

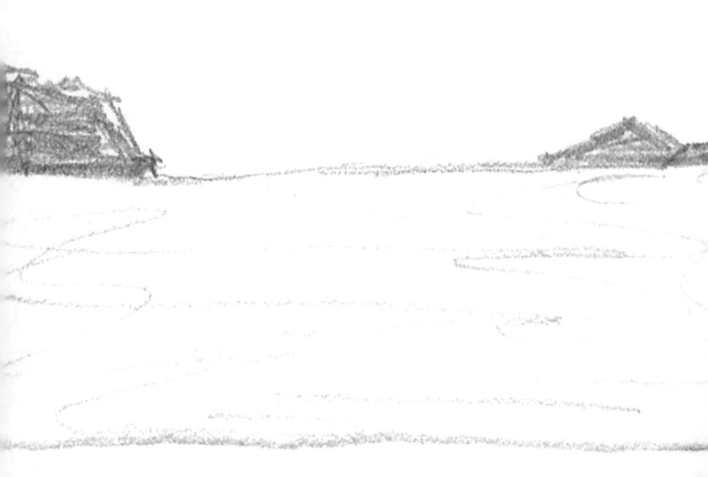

your eyes are fading
how still you are
your skin is breathing

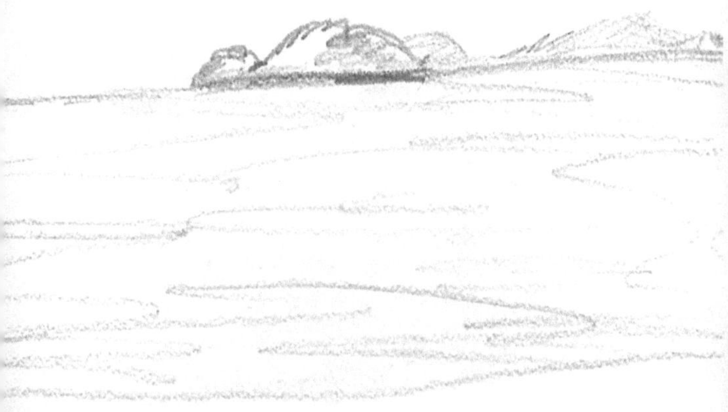

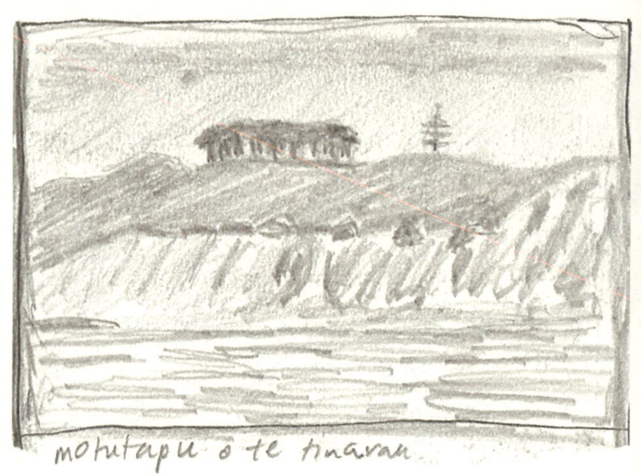

I wonder what I am doing
leaving you

I buy some peppermints

it begins to rain
8.45 boat

soft rain
constantly moving
concentric patterns
on the black cement

small congregations
of dark clothed people
huddle in the shelter
waiting

charcoal

willow tree

compressed extra soft

the wharf lights
like praying mantis
reflect outwards

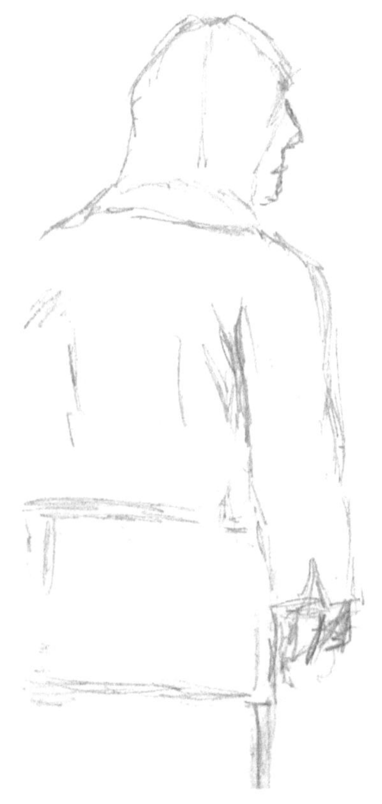

a white totem
ribboned and spiralling
into the darkness

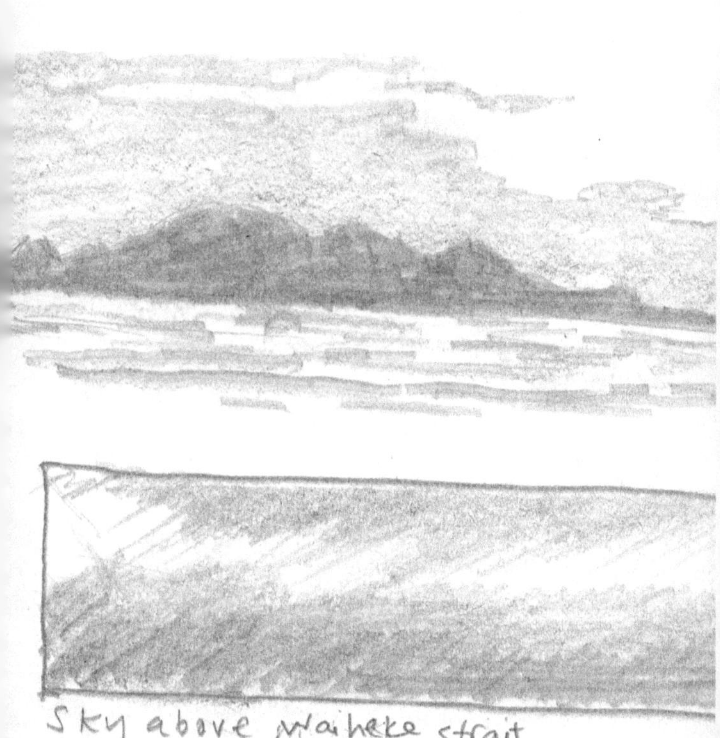

Sky above Waiheke Strait.

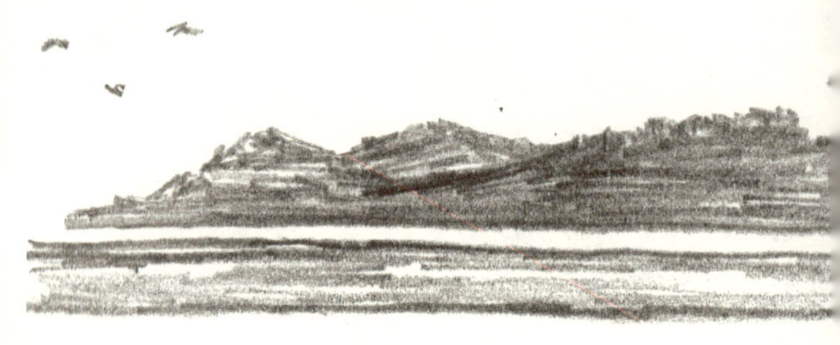

first the day

is bright

skuas
I like the light on the water
this morning the dark lights
the lines I mean dark lines
particularly near the horizon

I am

not there

graphite

sandpaper the graphite

walk through the

strike of the sun

there is a small space
between the chair and the table
to push my legs
into

the ferry leaves

different views into the strait

fade into conversation

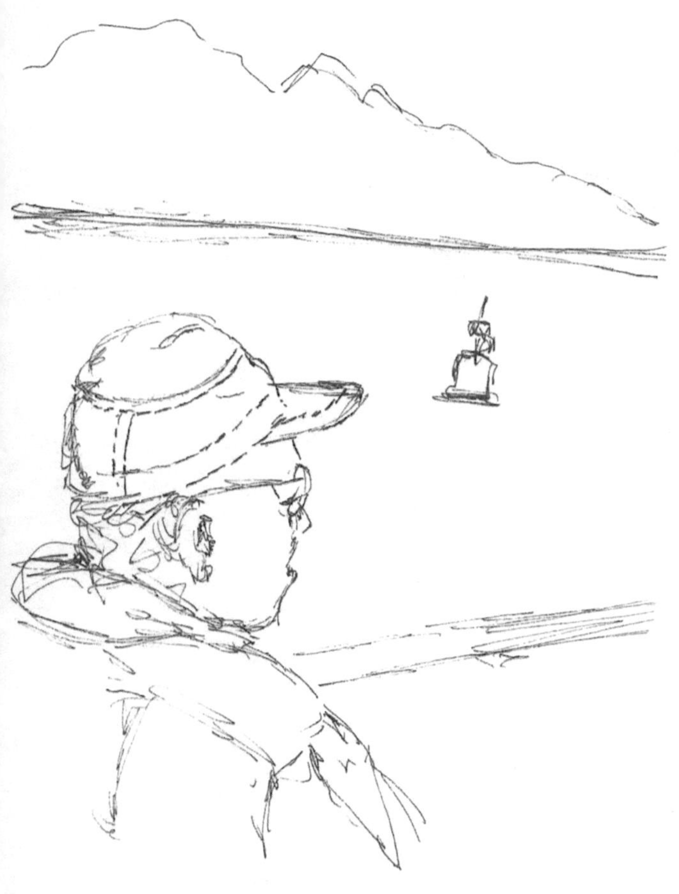

3 p.m ferry outside many people
older from the States and
Britain.

coming to browns island.
seems further away.

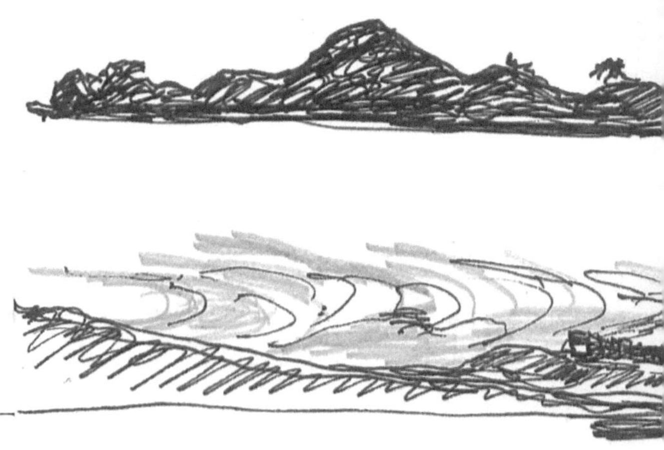

red cloud.

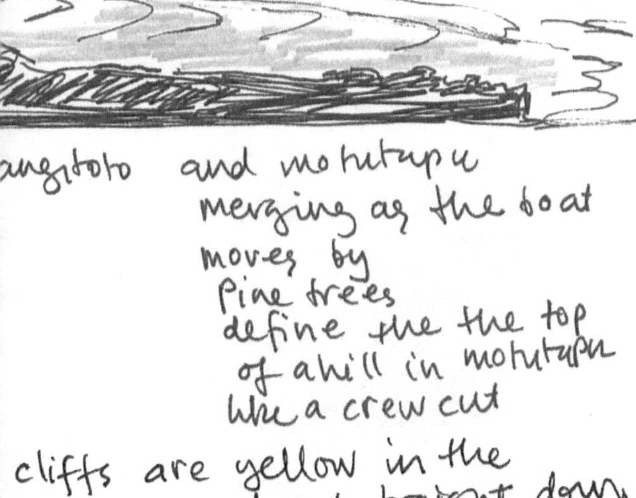

rangitoto   and motutapu
            merging as the boat
        moves by
            pine trees
            define the the top
            of a hill in motutapu
            like a crew cut
cliffs are yellow in the
            day / straight down.

Acknowledgement

I would like to acknowledge Daniela Gast for her thoughtful design, fusing words and images.

www.ingramcontent.com/pod-product-compliance
Lightning Source LLC
Chambersburg PA
CBHW032128050726
47590CB00008B/3009